Finding God
between
the Lines

Finding God between the Lines

*New Insights
from Familiar
Passages
and Places*

Jody Seymour

Judson Press ® Valley Forge

Finding God between the Lines: New Insights from Familiar Passages and Places

© 1997 Judson Press, Valley Forge, PA 19482-0851

Bible quotations in this volume are from the Revised Standard Version of the Bible, copyright © 1946, 1952, 1971, by the Division of Christian Education of the National Council of the Churches of Christ in the U.S.A. Used by permission.

Library of Congress Cataloging-in-Publication Data

Seymour, Jody, 1947—
    Finding God between the lines : new insights from familiar passages and places
    / Jody Seymour.
        p.   cm.
    ISBN 0-8170-1269-9 (pbk. : alk. paper)
    1. Christian life—Miscellanea.   I. Title
    BV4515.2.S49   1997
    242—dc21   97-14980

Printed in the U.S.A.

05 04 03 02 01 00 99 98 97

10 9 8 7 6 5 4 3 2 1

To Esther Seymour, my mother,
who now gets to ask Jesus
questions face-to-face

and

to my grandmother, Hattie Smith—

both helped me to find "God between the lines"

Contents

Part 2. The Christian Year
Advent, Christmas, and Epiphany

Lent and Easter

Part 3. The Old Story: From a Different Angle

Introduction

Sometimes the meaning of life is not found in the first reading. Purpose and reality are often found between the lines. What follows in this book is a search for God between the lines.

Many of the pieces in Part 1 are offered as reflections on everyday occurrences in life. Epiphanies of the Divine in the midst of life are more common than we may at first imagine, but we must first have eyes to see.

Other reflections are centered on scriptural scenes, and biblical characters are viewed from "around the corner." I have observed that stories and characters in Scripture can become like certain relatives at a family reunion: they are not really listened to because everyone already knows what they are going to say. I find that imagination is a wonderful tool for re-seeing and re-hearing the old, old story. I use the same approaches in Part 2 to explore some of the Scripture lessons that we hear during the celebration of the Christian church year.

I use poetry in many of the pieces in Parts 1 and 2. For me poetry is the language of the soul, the language of "between the lines." It is what one writes when words are not able to contain the full meaning of what is to be expressed. Poetry tries to get at what can't quite be gotten at. And often the prose *on* the lines needs the poetry of *between* the lines to help us see the familiar and experience the ordinary.

It sometimes takes a poet's eyes and ears to understand what another poet means, but I have attempted to make the poetry in this volume as understandable as any language of the soul can be. With some poetry that I attempt to read, I am forced to wonder if I have a soul that is being spoken to—the language leads me down a path of no return; I get lost in the words. Maybe I have a simple soul. You will not find "roses are red" poetry here, but neither will you find hard-to-follow verse that leads to ever darker places where no light seems to enter. I hope you find the poetry inviting as you make your way on your soul's journey.

In Part 3 I tell stories based on "the story." You will find familiar characters here, but again I have read between the lines of the stories. Sometimes I have taken the bright light of the Scripture and attempted to see what lies in the shadows. At other times all we have are thin shadows of certain figures within Scripture.

What did Cain think after the murder of Abel? How did Bathsheba feel about her part in David's self-made plight? What about the pathos of a Hosea having to deal with his prostitute wife? What kind of man taught the young Jesus? How did Simon of Cyrene feel about being made to carry the cross of Jesus? These and other questions are asked as some of the figures of Scripture are viewed "between the lines." Stand near the edge of the shadows and see some of these characters in a new light.

I hope that as you read these meanderings of my soul you will be able to catch a glimpse of God between the lines and perhaps gain some new understanding of this God whose ways are as mysterious as they are providential. We, like Moses, may desire to see God's face, only to be told by the Divine that we will be lucky to catch a glimpse of God's coattails. Yet somewhere within the labyrinthine ways of God, the person with eyes of faith can glimpse meaning.

So read between the lines. I offer you an old saying to bid you good journey: "Between the soul and God there is no between."

Part I

*Reflections on Scripture
and on Life*

Angels

Somewhere between the lines
    are the unspoken words.
Tucked amidst the rush of time
    there breathes the whisper.

Unseen messengers smile as their
    invisible presence surrounds us,
Made known only by the slightest
    notice of the eyes of the heart.

Sometimes they rest upon the shoulders
    of those who seem like strangers.
Quickly they go to those who are lost,
    who feel so alone.

They often spend moments of eternity
    with one who refused their help.
One dark afternoon they reached to him,
    but he turned his head away.

From a cross he whispered, "Later,"
    and they waited between the lines.
And now they are everywhere, released
    by the whisper of his love.

Look
    Listen
        find the lost spaces . . .
    There . . . there . . . are angels.

A Sandwich Communion

Her white hair was pulled back tightly so that the lines on her face were clearly visible for all to see. She commented to her companion seated across the table from her that the sandwich she was eating was surprisingly good. They had discussed the menu and had laughed earlier about the section titled "For Seniors."

They talked about the past, the traffic, and how they should see each other more often. The difficulty of cooking for just one was a final topic.

It was a sandwich communion—two lives brought together over some bread, some memories, and some hope. Most of the pages of these two women's lives had already been turned. As I overheard their conversation from my nearby table, I imagined children gone and husbands buried. Around their table that day they shared the life that was left to them.

"As often as you eat and drink . . . remember," Jesus said one evening to his friends sharing some bread around a table. He would soon do something that would make it difficult for them to forget.

But we do forget. We see a sandwich as simply lunch while all around us there is the longing for communion. We are surrounded by lives that need to be brought together like so much meat and bread. Preoccupied with our own fast-food style of life, we fail to listen and see.

Bread is broken all around us. Look. Listen. There is the possibility of a sandwich communion almost every day.

"Be Still . . ."

For whom do we wait when we wait on the Divine? Do we really want the mystery to surround us with its power?

Who is this God for whom we wait—

> a cosmic tease
> a testing father
> a curious mother
> a questioning friend
> one who waits for us to wait?

Is there something to the waiting itself? Is the anticipation part of the power of faith?

Like the food that must be waited for, is the hunger meant to drive us deeper to the place of our need?

Turning our attention away ceases the waiting. Then we search for other longings to fill us up, only to find that we must again wait, this time farther away from the last waiting place.

Stop.

Wait.

Waiting is the first step of faith.

Our God waits on our waiting. Such love is worth the wait.

The Sacred Relic

I tried simply to imagine where the steps used to be. Progress had torn down my grandfather's house. Where the back porch had been there were yellow stakes marking the path for the new highway that would soon be built. Beside the yellow stakes was a patch of purple wildflowers marking the grave of my memories.

The pecan trees still reached out their arms as if to provide shade for a dwelling that was no longer there. To a stranger the trees would have been merely trees on a vacant lot, but to the little boy who had grown up under their shade they looked painfully lonely.

My grandfather, whom I named "Paw Put," had watched me play under those trees. He had spit tobacco juice on their exposed roots as if to encourage their growth. The trees had responded. Now the arching limbs seemed to be waiting for some purpose that had been left behind.

As I looked down at the sand beneath my feet, I saw a piece of red-stained wood sticking up out of the Mississippi terrain. It was the only remnant of Paw Put's house. I picked up the fragment of wood and brushed the clinging sand from its weathered edges. This would be my relic.

Much like the early Christian pilgrims, I would keep this relic as a tiny piece of my past. This would be my equivalent of saints' bones to remind me of the sacred past.

Paw Put and the house are gone. The trees wait and watch for the coming of a paved future. But I shall, in a rather silly fashion I suppose, keep somewhere in the accumulations of my life a worn piece of wood to remind me of the love born in the shade. No highway can take me away from that place.

What are your sacred relics? Reach into your own heart and pull from your past a relic of love that has been invested with sacred worth. Somewhere trees were planted for your shade. We are all called to plant trees now that will be someone else's shade later.

Thank you, Paw Put, for though you and your house are gone, the lot of my soul is not vacant.

6

Open Hands

White like the fire's edge
are my gripping fingers
as I hold
to
what is mine.
If I let go I will lose
and fall into some
emptiness
that
will not hold me.
I will build storehouses
to keep the keeping
of my life,
and then
I will be sure.
But you say my soul
cannot hold it
without forfeit,
and I slip
beneath your love's weight.
Bury me then in the granary
of your grace and pry
open my clenched hands
to receive
what I cannot make.

Stir in my soul, O God, the power
found only in
letting go,
and give me freedom
from my bondage.

O God of the open hands,
store up in me
that which I cannot keep
that I may worry only about
loving you more.

Your Child First

(A Kind of Psalm)

O God, bend down and listen,
    for our breath has left us;
    we can but whisper.
Do not turn away because of
    our words of hurt and anger
    and longing.
Where do our children go?
Was she beyond your reach?
Where were the cradling arms that
    we needed to be there
    when ours could not be?
O God, are you not the protector
    of our children?

Are we screaming into a vast ocean,
    seeing only a distant
    horizon that seems to
    be too far away?
O God, let the waters wash over
    our naked feet and
    touch us from the distance.

Assure us that your heart is broken,
    for she was your child first.

She was known to you before we
    named her our name.
It was your spirit that filled her
    with the life we loved.

She was your child first.

Where were your hands to keep
    her from harm?
O listen to us in our brokenness.

9

Judge not our shaken faith.
Somehow we still turn to you,
   believing
   she was your child first.

And from the shadow cast in
      the midst of sun and clouds
      there comes a distant thunder
      and a voice,
"She was my child first—
         Did you not hear the word
         of long ago in a place where
         animals were sheltered?

         Did you not hear Mary weep
         from her labor and her joy?

         Did you not hear me proclaim
         'He is my child first'?

So soon I lost him
      to the loneliness of his cross,
And that day I heard the voices
      shouting from the shore
      asking, 'Where are you?
      Was he not your child?'

Listen well, all my children,
When harm surrounds, I am there
      though I do not hold back
      the tide that seems
      to take away your
         sons and daughters.
I am not the God beyond the
      horizon.
I am on the shore with you,
      broken with you.
I am bent down.
I am listening.

Look closely, see the scars.
My love like yours
has its wounds.

She was my child first.

I shall finish what was unfinished.
Though my power seems in this
instant not enough for you,
I am God.
I will bring life from death.

I was with her in that moment
when the waters surrounded her
and she seemed lost to you.

I am there when no one seems to be.
I am God.

The script is not as you have
written it.
It never is.
I alone see beyond the horizon.
I love you beyond the horizon.
I always will.

For you, for her
I shall bring life from death.
Death is mine as well as life.
I know your hurt.
I give you the salve of my
own healing.
It is my love created on a
dark hill long ago
when it seemed love
had died and gone beyond
the horizon.
I have bent down.
I do hear.

She was my child first.
And each of you—
   parent
   son
   daughter—
      You are my
         child first."

Whisper across Eternity

(Written after my mother's unexpected death)

Quietly you stepped to the
    other side,
Still smiling from joys
    held dear.
You seemed to slip from the
    grasp of my arms,
But you did not fall, for
    other arms held you.

The book beside the chair was
    not finished,
And there was other love I had
    to give to you.
But you are held by one who
    completes lives
    when books go unfinished.

What is it like?
Whisper across eternity, and
    I shall listen
    and tell others.

Is it my imagination that
    speaks as I hear a word—
    wonderful?
Is it simply wishful thinking,
    or an angel's voice?

It matters not, for hope is
    built not on whispers
    that I hear while
    tears teach me of
        joy and sadness.

The hope comes from one
    who closed the
    distance for a moment
    and spoke of "many rooms"
      and prepared places.

Say something to him for me;
    face to face I mean.
Ask now those questions
    we often asked
    of life and death,
    and finally rejoice
    in the answers.

Let him hold you close,
    he who held death so close
    that it became friend
    and no longer stranger.

Thank you for love given,
    for whatever stirs within me
    to write these words
    comes in part from your
    life and now your death.

Have a good time . . .
    we will talk later.

Grandmother Time

Grandmother Time sweeps, in preparation
for another age to come.
Children whose memories are as
shallow as a fresh rain pool
await the smell
of unseen tradition.

So it is with Time, the grandmother
preparing for her children.
We live in a house of memories
that we can listen to only
from squeaking rocking chairs
and in old stories.

Sit awhile, child of God,
and listen to Grandmother Time's
sweeping.
Moments are gifts prepared like
fresh, hot muffins in her
oven of ages past . . .
forget not to taste.

Granddaddy's Lesson

Gentle, like a Granddaddy
    long-legged spider
Walking softly across my porch.
Can I walk across life like
    that?

Touching the surface but disturbing
    little beneath my feet.
No clamor, but stepping as if my
Cadence was but a faint
    whisper.

From ledge to ledge I would reach;
    the created touching the creation.
Part of life, yet above it.
So light my movement that some would
    miss me.

Yet like the spider I would be seen
    by unknown eyes
Who watched me gently touch life,
Though slight of step, my every move
    counted.

Granddaddy teaches a silent lesson
    for those who will see,
Of life and the gentle meaning of even
Our slightest steps as they are
    watched by God
        of spider
        and
        of me.

The Wrinkle in Jesus' Face

Dark were his eyes as he
cooled my face,
Given by people who managed death.
But I remember life
and the wrinkle
in Jesus' face.

Some funeral home provided them—a subtle way of advertising in church. Before the days of air conditioning it was those funeral-home fans with the face of Jesus printed on them that kept sweaty believers cool.

Jesus was constantly on the move during those sultry evenings of my childhood. Like a field of flowers tossed about by the breeze, those paper images of Jesus gave comfort to the faithful.

I remember that often the well-used fans would have a wrinkle running right across Jesus' face, a scar telling of how frequently that gentle picture had been needed. Perhaps Jesus had been wedged between two hymnals by a child who had turned the instrument of redemption from heat into a kind of springboard. Those wooden handles made such interesting sounds if thumped just the right way.

His face is gone now as we sit so still in church, cooled by efforts not our own. Could it be that we need some old funeral-home fans to remind us of the need to face Jesus again? Too distant are the reminders of the wrinkles in his face, the scars on his hands, and the sweaty reality of his love for us.

Dew Child

She was dressed in her Sunday best. The pink dress with the lace collar was matched by shiny white shoes.

As she walked toward her destination in the front yard of her brown frame house, the backdrop for this picture, I could see her flicking the dew from the grass with her tiny white shoes.

The mother who had picked out those shoes might have chastised her for getting them wet, but for now this child was alone on her journey. Her destination was a moisture-covered plastic bag resting on the front lawn. The transparent pouch contained the Sunday morning newspaper.

As she picked up the paper, she seemed to pay little attention to the package. She was lost in the dew and its wonder.

I was in the midst of my Sunday morning run when I was graced with the sight of this dew child. As she threw the plastic bag over her shoulder, I noticed that the paper was more than half the size of her petite frame.

Did she not know what it was that she innocently carried over her tiny shoulder? Within that package were headlines of murder, starvation, political corruption, and even the heaviness of the obituaries. Wrapped in her moist container was the news of a big world now on the shoulder of this little dew child.

Waiting to be unfolded from her parcel were the advertisements of all the items that consumers must have in order to be fulfilled. Tucked in the bag were pages filled with the names of people who were longing so much to find another person that they had called out in print from the "personals" section.

She did not know. All she knew was that there was something wet and shiny on the Sunday morning grass that was worth kicking with her "church" shoes.

Remind me, O God, that in the midst of all the heavy headlines, the things I have to have, and the crying out of "personal" desires, there is dew to kick. And for that un-named dew child, I pray that as she grows and begins to read and comprehend the contents of her package, she will some-where in the recesses of her mind and soul remember how to kick the sparkling moisture from the grass.

Thank you, child of the morning. Thank you for kicking some dew my way.

Those Demons

How simple it would be if they were creatures with claws unfurled, holding onto us with fiendish grasp, but those are childhood nightmares. The demons that take hold of us are wiser than storybook monsters. They survey our souls, plotting where they shall build their dwellings within us.

They are pretty parasites that slowly take away our spirit's life. They leave us with smiling faces concealing empty hearts, hearts that sense that they have given themselves to something that is not sacred.

But there is one who walks the narrow streets of our lives listening to the voices. He knows our demons' names, though they hide behind our fleshy veils. He hears their whispers and their shouts. After listening he says but a phrase reflecting a victory already won: "Be silent!"

The demons always listen, for they know his voice. We are the ones who have trouble hearing.

Trust and Obey

Was she lost, or had she in fact found something to help her down the rough path of growing old? She walked by me, humming to herself and to anybody who wanted to hear. Her song leaped from a body that could barely shuffle. The notes were projected in crisp, clear "dee-dee-dee-dees."

I recognized the tune as she passed by me. "Dee, dee, dee, dee, dee, dee." Anyone who had been brought up going to church at least three times a week as a child could recognize those "dee dees" as

> When we walk with the Lord,
> In the light of his love,
> What a glory he sheds on our way.
> While we do his good will,
> He abides with us still,
> And with all who will trust and obey.

So the translation of the "dee dees" was that old hymn "Trust and Obey." She was singing her way through the narrow passages of the maze called old age. There, in a nursing home chapel surrounded by heads that drooped down toward wheelchairs, came the rusty notes echoed through aging pipes, "dee, dee, dee, dee, dee, dee."

Her way of coping was to "dee dee" herself through the remaining years. She could no longer remember the words. They were shelved in the back corners of her mind behind names and faces that were also out of reach. But the tune was available, and somehow she knew how to "trust and obey."

We had all better learn some tunes, no matter what our age. Certain songs will serve us well as we walk farther down the road. It is easy to get lost if we walk far enough, but there is one who never quits looking for us. This dear lady found him somewhere on her journey. They walk together now down the halls of a nursing home singing, "dee, dee, dee, dee, dee, dee . . . When we walk with the Lord."

21

Children All Are We

(A Kind of Affirmation)
I am a child of God.
I need love in order to grow.
I have fears that I may not be able to
tell you about.
I have at times failed in my loving,
but I know the power of love.
I have felt forgiveness, both divine
and human, and know of its healing.

I need other people.
I need other people to laugh with me.
I need other people to cry with me
or at least to be with me when I cry.
I need to know that people love me enough
to tell me when they think I am wrong
and forgive me in my wrongdoing.
I need to know that love is there even though
the loving may be the denial of
what I think I need.

I need to know that I am accepted as
the child I am no matter what my age.
I need others' love to remind me that
I find myself as I give myself and
not just by finding myself.
I need love to remind me that, like a child,
if left alone I will be selfish.

I need others to help remind me of
the lost—
the spiritually lost
the financially lost
the socially lost
the lost—

for I have been or will be lost,
and I want someone to be interested
in finding me.
I am a child . . . and yes, I know that I am expected
to be strong, for that is what growing
up is about.
But I am also a child of God,
whose only boy came and exposed
his own weakness and vulnerability
because that is what it took
to really love.

So I confess and profess that
we need not be so troubled,
for
children all are we.

Thou Preparest a Table

(I wrote this poem after the annual Kindermourn Christmas memorial service. Kindermourn is an organization whose purpose is to support parents who have lost children to death. At this service, parents come forward and speak the name of their child who has died, light a candle, and place the candle on the table.)

O God, what is this table full
of the light of death?
So many flickering candles,
each a life gone out.

How much pain is on that table, God?
tears like wax, on the table.
Struggling voices speak names,
precious memories placed
on that table.

What will you do with the candles, God?
their light bears witness
That there is too much darkness
in your world of promise.

You must prepare another table, God.
somewhere beyond our pain,
Where those whose names are spoken
light candles for themselves,
and for us who weep now.

Around that table there is no pain,
but there is laughter,
For there are children playing
in the light of a love
unmatched by any.

But at our table, we must still prepare,
for we must laugh again,
And our bleeding wax and our faltering

voices allow us to remember
that we might live.

How big your table must be, God,
but at your table
What is unfinished shall be finished,
So until we gather around
your lighted table . . .
O God,
help us to prepare our table.

It's Only Bread

It's only bread,
Does love taste like this?
Should not honey be dripped
    over the waiting crust?

It's only bread,
No feeling in textured wheat.
The loaf now torn seems
    only broken nurture.

It's only bread,
Until he says, "Take and eat,"
And makes the morsel a memory
    of a meal and a cross.

It's only bread,
But in its taste is a promise
That love's as real as torn bread,
    eaten in remembrance.

It's only bread,
But as I draw near to kneaded love,
Somehow I am a child with a
    place at the table.

Not Hungry

The father gave his son the piece of bread that had been torn from the loaf for him. I was leaning over to the kneeling father and son to offer them the communion cup. The young boy handed the bread back to his father with a three-word reply: "I'm not hungry."

Sometimes we are starving when we come to God. Our lives are empty, having been filled too much with the "stuff" of life, which does not really nourish us. We know that we need something, even if we do not know what it is. Much like children, we need to be fed, but we do not know what is good for our health. At times like these we need to be spoon-fed from the Lord's table.

But then there are times when we come not feeling particularly hungry. There is no burning need, no huge space to be filled. We come bringing no appetite for what God wants to give us. At this moment we are in danger of missing something that might be good for us.

Often times we are "not hungry" because we have been filled with bite-sized pieces from other tables. Our appetites deceive us into imagining that we do not need anything from God's menu.

At times like these we need to be careful. What God offers promises to nourish us unlike any fast food from life's buffet. Our stomachs have become accustomed to filling up on what is available; our palates crave what seems to taste good at the time. Sometimes we are not hungry when it comes time for God to do the feeding.

Go to the table anyway . . . even when you do not think you are hungry.

Healing

Torn like pieces of dry cloth with
frayed edges dangling—

Broken like fragments of
once-fine china—

Empty like that childhood
cookie jar—

Lost like the traveler whose
map was left at home—

Hurting like the deep pain
of a first love lost—

Dying like a flower delivered
but now solitary and limp—

Touch us, O God, whose boy's
hands were
torn
broken
empty
lost
hurt
and lifeless
for us.

Jonah

I tried to hide from his ways, but even the tempest found me. Troubled were the waves but no more troubled than my tossed soul. I wanted to be lost if being found meant changing the course of my life.

What kind of God would feed me to the deep to fill his hunger? He was a tease who would spill me onto some forgotten shore only to lead me down a path that I did not want to travel . . . just because it was his way.

Divine guidance seemed to me like a mysterious fish who swallowed me whole. My plans and my life were consumed by a God of fish and folk. This God must love to play with his creatures.

Go ahead and flee from him. Swim if you must, for he may choose to swallow you up in the ever-reaching grasp of some scaly angel of the deep that comes from the very recesses of your own hiding, crying soul.

He will find you . . . this God who loves to fish.

O Father

(Tradition has it that Jesus' earthly father, Joseph, died before Jesus began his active ministry. The Bible does not mention Joseph during the active years of Jesus' life. I wonder how Jesus must have felt as he prepared to bury his "father.")

> O father, how cold you are,
>   no longer the warmth of
>   that hand that taught me
>   the use of chisel and hammer.
> You held me on the long nights
> when mother grew too tired
>   to hold me when I was in need
>   of being held.
>   O father, mentor and friend.
>
> I am still struggling with the power
>   within those same hands that you
>   carefully guided when I was so young.
> Could these hands now give you life
>   much as you brought life to the wood?
>
> O father, you knew I had another father,
>   yet you cared not, for I was yours
>   though not of your flesh.
> But now, your flesh is cold and lifeless,
>   and I stand here seemingly helpless.
> Is my unwillingness . . . my helplessness
>   reflected in mother's eyes,
>   or is that simply grief?
>
> O father, I am not yet ready to offer
>   this strange warmth of healing,
>   a soon-to-be burning in my flesh.
> In moments the flame almost consumes
>   me with passions that seem beyond.
> I must seek some wilderness to wander
>   that I might discover what to do

with this burning.
But for now, O father, I release you
    into the hands of another one
    whom I also call "Abba."
Take my father, O Abba, and shape
him anew as he once shaped the
    cradle in which I slumbered.
Hold him again as your child,
for his leaving hurts me.

O father, I cannot help you just now,
    but soon I will live into this dying
    that you now do.

O father, I let you go gently into
    another's arms who will hold you
    even more tenderly than you
    held me on those long nights.

I faintly remember those arms as
    if it was some distant dream.
But they are waiting, O father
    . . . they are waiting.

Render to Caesar

"What shall we do, good teacher?" they asked as they set the trap. "Caesar's head is upon it. How much of it is his?"

Jesus twirled the coin between his calloused fingers. The questioners thought for a moment that perhaps some magic would be done to the simple coin.

A pensive Caesar for a moment lay captive in the hands of this one whom some called the Son of God. Did Caesar know that what was "his" was soon to be challenged by another king?

Those who asked the question already knew what was God's. Jesus glanced their way and told them to render according to who owned what.

Whose kingdom takes in whose? They were left with the question. Jesus tossed the coin heavenward. It landed flat in his hand. He smiled and tossed it their way, the coin and the question.

Could it be that the coin and the question are still in the air, coming our way?

Weeds

He ran the soft kernels through his fingers as would a child who played with blades of grass. Tomorrow's bread, resting gently in his hands. But today it was only a few shafts of wheat he had picked from a field.

His earlier words had reminded them of daily bread, but they were so concerned about the anxieties of the future that he knew they did not really hear. Now they were asleep, and he was alone by a dying fire, remembering their remarks.

Matthew had wanted to know why the weeds were allowed to grow with the wheat. Judas had grown angry with the very story. He wanted to know why there could not be a harvest now. Only Peter's insistence that Judas leave the argument to another time had caused the matter to be dropped.

Now Jesus was alone, the wheat cradled in his hands. He looked into the disciples' sleeping faces and remembered his own final words: "Leave the weeds to the final harvest."

He had selected such an assortment of men to be his disciples. How he now wished to do some selective weeding, but his own words hung heavy around him like the evening dampness.

His head found a place on his earthen bed. Looking toward the stars, he closed his eyes and whispered, "Thy will be done."

Temptation

Stones, God, could they be bread,
my soul and body ache,
both seem empty.
Fill me, if only with the
rushing wind as it blows
over these dry stones.

Quickly, for he speaks again
of power that can be
mine for the asking.
Hold me, before I raise my
hands to see if angels
would bear me up.

Kneeling, I honor not him but
you who drove me into this
barren place of trial.
Drown me again, this time
with the unseen waters
of your cleansing love

. . . and baptize my temptations.

Heaven and Hell

Fires of long ago remind the listener
    of the hell of indifference.
But Heaven's open door waits for
    bridges to be built across the chasm.

Eternity's lingering cry that "no one
    would listen to a voice of resurrection"
Waits for a reply from those who
    now claim the name of the Christ.

Christ is alive, but so is poor Lazarus,
    for Hell is reflected in the struggler's face.
Pass not by the wounded ones, O traveler.
    We are Heaven's children, not Hell's puppets.

He who slammed Hell's door now cries,
    "I am the naked stranger. . . ."
Heaven and Hell met one Friday at a crossroad
    and we must separate the two.

Sanctuary

The loneliness felt good. So many hands had been reaching out to him, hands that had been empty for so long. Those hands wanted as much of him as he could give, but after so much giving he felt empty.

Tossing a small stone toward the darkness, he smiled, wondering how far down the slope his disciples must be after missing him. "Serve me, and I will make these stones bread." Those words still echoed in his memory. But this morning he needed some nourishment not simply for his tired body. He needed something to fill the hollow place in his spirit.

Praying on the run was not enough. Some moments like these were needed to allow God to renew him—moments to breathe deeply. Much was still left to do, much more left to give. He often dreamed of empty hands.

His solitude was broken. "Where in God's name have you been?" His precious silence was now tossed into the morning as the stone had been earlier. "They are all looking for you. What do you want me to tell them?"

Jesus reached for Peter's empty hand and pulled himself up from his place of rest. He took one last deep breath and motioned to his discoverer. "I'm coming, my friend. Did I leave you alone so long?"

Jesus allowed Peter to walk a few steps ahead; then he turned and looked over his shoulder one last time at the place of his brief sanctuary. As he walked down the mountain, he lifted his head and spoke gently into the breeze, "Thank you."

Alone in the Crowd

Matthew's mind wandered back to
  days of the stale but steady
    security of the tax table.
Peter dreamed of long yet fulfilling
  days of nets cast not for people
    but for fish caught and sold.

John wondered if his youthful days of
  loving would wear thin, for life now
    was becoming too heavy, too quick.

Andrew remembered the starry-eyed
  days of romance and promises made
    to a young girl now faded from memory.

James reached into his soul for days
  of beginnings when excitement filled
    their minds rather than fear and doubt.
Their minds were tired from too many
  days of surprise and promised crosses,
    and now it was night.
So except for Judas, who felt the days
  had run out, they slept
    beneath the olive trees.
Though his plea to watch and pray
  still was remembered, the days were long,
    and the only escape seemed sleep.
And Jesus knew how hard it had been
  for them and their dreams,
    so he knelt to pray, alone.

What a Convention

What would it have been like if there had been political conventions in Jesus' day?

Imagine . . .

Press release: *The Palestine Gazette*

There was quite a floor fight over the party platform at last week's convention of the newly formed Christian Party. The diversity of the delegates made the disagreements over the future direction of the party inevitable. One political observer stated recently, "Those Christians are made up of every kind of person imaginable. There seems to be no defining principle as to whom they allow in."

Simon Peter, majority leader, suggested that the party platform take a middle-of-the-road approach. His contention was that too many radical ideas at such a critical time would alienate the people.

It looked as if the majority position would win the day until the party leader, Jesus of Nazareth, gave the keynote speech of the convention. Near the beginning of his speech he was interrupted many times by applause and cheers. It was obvious that his party was overjoyed to have him as their leader. The new Christian Party seemed to have many people in its ranks who had lost hope of anything new happening in Palestine.

The shouts and cheers quickly ceased, however, when Jesus began outlining his plan for the party's future. This plan involved unbelievable risks and sacrifices. A few delegates were seen leaving even before his speech was concluded. They rose from their seats after Jesus mentioned praying for enemies and giving away huge amounts of one's resources to the poor. Complete silence engulfed the convention as the Christians' leader suggested that he might even have to die to get his program across to the people.

The convention ended rather abruptly when it was realized that the party leader was not going to conform to the wishes of most of the delegates. It remained to be seen what would become of the fledgling group. It seemed that even

Jesus' closest advisors did not agree on the direction the party should take.

Jesus suggested that because things were going the way they were, he should take his case to the people at the yearly gathering in Jerusalem. Latest word is that none of his advisors agree.

In this writer's opinion, the new Christian Party is not only dropping in the recent polls but does not stand a chance in the general election. Its platform and its leaders are much too radical for times such as these.

Part 2

The Christian Year

Advent, Christmas, and Epiphany

Advent

Before the evergreen of hope there appears the wilderness of waiting. We desire to pour some water down our throats quickly, but first our thirst must be noticed.

"No one knows the hour of his coming," go the ancient words with dusty sounds. And so we hurry around the "end" and create our own jingle-bell beginnings.

But the birth requires a waiting, unless it is a molded plastic baby that we really desire. The unwrapped manger child is not the real thing. Remember.

Only through the Advent wilderness, where thirsty pilgrims journey, can the child who comes "out back" be found and rediscovered to be ours. Remember.

The Creator of all time still holds the ends and wonders if we will take the time to prepare a highway for a king who has come to take something away before he gives. Remember.

The waiting wilderness leaves us dry so that later we may truly taste the water. Those who want to be pilgrims and not simply be passersby need to not hurry by the Advent wilderness. In such haste the Christmas child will be missed. Remember.

A Prayer Not to Get Lost This Advent

O God, I can already hear people complaining. They use your name in a strange sort of way:

"O God, I'll be glad when Christmas is over."

We get lost almost every year at this time, God.

Lost trying to remember . . .
Lost trying to buy our way out . . .
Lost trying to finish the list . . .
Lost trying to make it the best Christmas ever.

Save us, God, as only you can do. Save us from the wilderness of malls, the wilderness of plastic, and the desert of re-creations of Christmas past.

Pull us aside and remind us that we must tiptoe to the manger if we are to hear the sounds of Christmas. He will come again, won't he?

Wrestle us away from the depression of not having enough

time
love
money.

Save us with the soft cry of the child who knows we still need silent nights.

You know how to find us when we are lost. Make us remember that what matters is love given.

And make us believe that if you help us not to get lost, we must help you find those this Advent who do get lost.

We pray in the name of the child who came for the lost child in all of us. Amen.

Advent Wilderness

Roads bending around the
    dryness of our souls.
A dripping wet messenger
    steps onto the path.
        "Prepare!"
What baptism is this you offer
    for our parched places?
Your water seems hot as if
    warmed by some judging fire.

Who is this one of whom you speak
    who shall wash and reap?
Is this not more arid wilderness—
    more rules like salt in our mouths?

Bathe us in spite of our fears—
    Other waters have left us waiting.
Fill our wilderness with your promise
    of one who is to come
        and we shall wait
            and wonder.

O Joseph

O Joseph, what is it you say,
no room for our child?
Do they know who it is
they turn away?

But of course they do not know,
for I barely know.
No angel prepares room
for the life within me.

Yet it is time, Joseph, so we
must find a place.
Take whatever is offered,
for my evening grows short.

This place will be fine, my love;
feel no remorse.
God must know something
unrevealed to you and me.

Sleep, Mary

Sleep now, Mary. Your labor of love is over. He is so beautiful, our Jesus. I will hold him as you sleep.

The lullaby I will sing to him will serenade the animals too. So sleep now, Mary, with the rest of tired Bethlehem.

Tomorrow's world will be different because of your work this night, Mary.

Look now at your sleeping mother, child. See how gentle is her brow. Do you know of the love that has birthed you this night? Your eyes seem to ask questions of me that I cannot answer.

Sleep, O child of God, and accompany your mother in her dreams of peace. My carpenter's hands hold such craft.

You were not of my making, child. An angel's breath formed you. God and your now-sleeping mother labored lovingly over your creation.

Sleep, child. Sleep, Mary. You will both wake to a world where dreams have come true.

The Whisper in the Night Breeze

I give you myself, O little one.
You lean against my breast
to taste our human plight.
Do you feel the dampness
in the night breeze?

A stable's noise, your first sounds.
Soft is your face in a hard world,
yet you seem to smile.
From across the dark hills I hear music
in the night breeze.

The message first came through an open window.
One evening in my emptiness the voice
said that you would come.
Some angel's whisper naming me to carry
the child of the night breeze.

Dear Joseph, you too heard the whisper.
In your fear you felt the dampness
of Love's voice in the air.
O God of angel voices,
what will become
of my child
of
the night breeze?

Epiphany

Footsteps follow some bright
   radiant beam,
But in the palace the king
   they seek is not there.

Seeking wisdom they find
   but a child,
Yet gifts are laid beside
   the manger king.

An old man, blind in his
   waiting, waits—
Smelling of incense, so long
   he has been in the temple.

Then he hears a name, "Jesus,"
   and he cradles the child,
Laughing, weeping, and singing
   his departure song of peace.

Thunder rolls above the Jordan
   as baptismal waters pour,
And the child, now man, hears
   the voice, "He is my son!"

A proud God shouts to a world
   whose deaf ears hear the joy,
And a dove descends upon
   one who is wet with love.

The wedding guests grow silent
   as the wine jars empty,
But the stranger from Nazareth
   offers water to those who will drink.

"Foolish man," some say as a
willing guest lifts the cup
And tastes the finest of wines,
firstfruits of God's own vineyard.
Epiphany . . .

Lent and Easter

Elements of Salvation

Green branches cut from
    their roots
Used as greetings for a new
    coming king.
Green branches never to grow
    again or wave in
    evening breezes.

A fresh towel once clean
    and spotless
Now spoiled with dirt from
    disciples' feet.
A fresh towel no longer new
    but now a servant's rag
    stained with love.

A new tomb hewn out of
    the waiting earth
Welcoming a silent king
    who washed feet.
A new tomb holding old promises
    for a moment made alive
    by a now-dead Jesus.

Green branches, a fresh towel,
    a new tomb—
The makings of God's surprise
    for sleeping disciples.
Branches, towels, tombs . . .
    elements of salvation
    in God's mysterious way.

A Voice in the Crowd

Don't push me. I came early just to see him for myself, this new king who talks of peace.

I'll not give up my place in front of the crowd. This too is my holiday. I want to see the reason for this parade.

Listen to the hosannas shouted by hungry people longing to be fed in this religious wilderness of ours. Hunger such as this is dangerous.

I'm here just to watch. There is nothing I can see to shout about in a land forgotten by a distant God.

So . . . he is what we have gathered in such numbers for . . . So small and riding on a beast of burden.

Here, stranger. You can now have my place in front. I waited for more than this.

How can he "save his people" with palm branches and donkeys and pensive smiles shared with a crowd?

It will take more than some parade to save the likes of us. God only knows what it will take . . .

He Died So Hard

(Thoughts of One of the Soldiers Who Crucified Jesus)

He died so hard,
    this misguided king.
His hands seemed to reach
    beyond the nails as
        if to hold on
            to some forgotten
                beauty.

So little for him to hold to
    after betrayal and denial.
Why would he want to grasp
    such emptiness in
        a kingdom awash
            in slippery subjects
                who claim him not?

He died so hard, until he
    lifted those tired, lonely eyes.
Then he seemed to see someone
    who was reaching down to him but
        who could not help him
            and make his dying easier
                in his last breath.

Those last words of "forgive
    them for not knowing."
O strange, forgotten king, we
    know exactly what we are
        doing and to whom we
            bow in allegiance,
                and it is not you.

Still, why do I feel your death,
   for you are but a number to me.
You give your spirit up to
   some father you do not see,
     and yet you die,
       a forgotten child
         of a far too distant god.

Why is it you die so hard?

The Stone Is Too Heavy

The stone's weight is too much for
life to overcome, so death is measured
in the stone's silent witness.

Like disciples' eyes but a few evenings
before, the portal is closed, and hope
has been put to sleep.

The grief of the world hung on his
shoulders as he died looking into the
heaviness of being forsaken.

Why go and face a stone that speaks
only of covered-over dreams that now
will never see the light of promise?

But what is this? The stone is laid aside
as though some unseen hand would not have
defeat be the last word spoken.

As I peer into the emptiness I feel his
forsakenness lingering like the early
morning dew escaping sun's light.

But who will roll away the stone from the
opening in my heart, now covered with
the mystery and questions?

O Lord, what is this you speak, that
no stone is too heavy nor weight
too burdensome that you
cannot move it?

Resurrection has rolled away the stone,
and life is made new under the mighty
weight of a God who will
not die.

Escape to Emmaus

Walk faster please, Cleopas. I want to escape the pain. Emmaus is not far now. There we can rest and forget.

Do not talk about him, Cleopas. His name leaves me so empty. I had so much hoped he was going to turn it all around.

Are you forgetting the cross, Cleopas? Hurry now. Let's leave it behind. This is some terrible dream. I want to wake up in Emmaus.

Who is this beside the road, Cleopas? He walks our way as if to join us. Pay him no attention, for I have nothing to share this day with a stranger.

Where are you from, nameless one, that you do not know of our sorrow? I felt the world knew of our emptiness, for even his tomb is now barren. We had hoped to avoid even your questions this day. Forgive our lack of hospitality, but you who seem not to know of our loss would not understand.

Yes, you heard us right. Even his tomb is barren. Who knows what it means? All we know is that he is gone. Our dream is but shattered reality.

What is this you say about our Scriptures? You know of our hopes then, at least in the old, forgotten promises. Yet never have I heard these old promises spoken of in such a lively manner . . . except one other time . . . but then . . .

We did not welcome you earlier, stranger. Forgive our blindness. Have some food with us and perhaps share more of your wisdom, for we are like starving, lonely children.

Yes, you . . . you break the bread as a sign of the hospitality we failed to show you along the road. O my God, the wounds, the hands. Only now do I see your face.

Master, how could I not have known? Is my grief so heavy?

Leave not again. But you do. Could it be that no tomb or expectation can hold you?

Cleopas, you smile. Did you know all along?

Hurry. We must go back . . . back to that place of cross and death . . . and shout into all the emptiness . . . shout that the breaker of bread, broken himself, is alive.

You Cannot Run to Emmaus

You cannot run to Emmaus;
you must walk.
Those first two followers
walked almost too slowly,
their feet weighed down
with grief.

But they walked slowly enough
to discover Jesus;
though they knew not
who it was that walked
with them, still they listened.

Today we who follow often
try to run to Emmaus.
We are in a hurry to accomplish
the important task,
and in our hurry we miss
on the road the very Jesus
whom we wish to follow.

So we must walk to Emmaus,
slowly enough to hear Jesus.
So many times we have arrived
at journey's end but missed him,
because in our hurry we failed
to hear and see our Lord.

Walk slowly, O pilgrim,
and listen to his words.
They are old words, heard before,
but they can be different
when you become aware that
Jesus speaks them
to you.

You cannot run to Emmaus.
Pause now and listen.
In your sorrow, he is there.
In your past joy, he was there,
and now on the road
he speaks to you again.

Somewhere on your journey,
your Lord will break bread.
If you but lift your eyes,
you will see him anew,
for he has been with you
all along the road.

Part 3

*The Old Story:
From a Different Angle*

You Can Run, but You Can't Hide

The leaves move beneath his feet. I can hear him coming. Hiding is new for me, but if I am very still, perhaps he will not hear me breathing. It has been such a little time since I first felt that breath rush into my shaking frame. Will he now take that breath from me? Will I be to him like the dust beneath his feet?

The choice was mine, but she offered the fruit in such an inviting way. Companionship has its price, and I was so lonely. Her soft body next to mine filled the emptiness of my days. For the first time I felt complete. Her gentle breath upon my chest as she slept was a gift from heaven to me.

I wanted to keep her beside me always, but she insisted on her freedom. She wanted to walk alone in the garden. Together we had walked beside that tree many times, and together we had shared the same thought. But we remembered his words of warning, though we did not understand the reason. Together we had been strong in our denial.

But now she has betrayed us both. She came to me with fruit in hand. I did not even have to ask from which tree she had taken it. I knew.

She told me it was not like any of the other fruit. Why did I not throw the half-eaten fruit to the ground and scold her for her wondering? Perhaps it was because I knew in that moment something she had never known. I knew what it felt like to be alone.

Could I now leave her alone in the judgment that must surely come? What would this meal cost? I gave away my freedom because I had it to give. I knew what I was doing.

As I bit into the fruit, I noticed her eyes. She had never looked at me this way before, even though never was not so long for us. It was then that I felt the chill of the air in the garden for the first time. The damp air seemed to cling to my naked body. The feeling was new and awful.

The pounding in my chest was frightening. So this was fear.

In that moment I saw it crawling on the ground beside us.

I had not seen it on the ground before. It had always been in one of the many trees in the garden, always watching us.

I grabbed her hand and started to run. In my haste I somehow let go of her hand. She must now be hiding separately from me somewhere in the garden. If I am quiet, perhaps I can hear her breathing, rapid as it must be from our escape.

But what is this I hear . . . my name being called. He is calling my name. I remember how he allowed me to name all that is in the garden. Now my name echoes amidst the animals that I named. No one will come to his bidding, for only I am Adam.

I shall offer my excuses: "She made me eat." But I know that it was not she who caused my hiding. She was created out of my loneliness. I cannot leave her alone now in her guilt. She knew somehow that I would not refuse her invitation to eat. Her blame is mine.

What will he do? I know now why the serpent crawls in the dust. O dust from which I came, cover me. There is such a chill in the air. Cover me.

A Marked Man

His mark is heavy. Though it spares my life, its weight causes me to walk as if I am carrying a heavy burden on my back. What kind of strange love is this? He lets me live, but my living becomes a sign of my guilt.

Eve loved him more than me. Even in the days of childhood it was Abel who made her smile. I did everything to win her approval. It is a curse not to be blessed.

To live without both my mother's blessing and God's was too much. I worked hard to produce good crops while Abel played with his stupid sheep. They were like children to him as he walked among them. Tears filled his eyes when he sacrificed one of his "children." Such a conflict of loves bothered my sensitive brother.

When I placed my firstfruits of the field on the altar, Abel was still weeping like some snotty-nosed child. I told him to "run to Momma," but he did not pay me any attention.

God's blessing I could have done without, but the reality of that weepy-eyed brother of mine receiving a divine blessing when I did not was more than I could take. I had worked long hours in the fields. My crops were plentiful. Why was I not favored?

Knowing my questioning heart, God felt my hidden sin. Do my motives have to be pure if the offering is given? Who is this God who wants the heart to be so pure?

Abel was not looking when I struck him. It would not have mattered, for I was stronger than he. I could have looked him in the eyes and told him what I was going to do, and he would have simply looked back at me with those shepherd's eyes of his.

I did not give him the pleasure of that last pastoral expression. I struck him the deadly blow from behind and left him at the altar of sacrifice. His blood mingled with the blood of his precious sheep.

There was sarcasm in the voice that found me. "Where is your brother, Abel?" he asked. God and I both knew where he was, so I threw the question back: "Am I my brother's keeper?"

There was no answer, just the mark . . . a mark that now keeps me alive. But this is no life. All know who I am by this mark. My crops spoil in the womb of the earth, and my labors produce only stillbirths.

I shall teach my children to despise this God who withholds blessings. I shall offer only sacrifices of bitter herbs on the altar if that is all he gives to me. The seeds of my loins will multiply the fruit of my bitterness. This God does not know what he has done.

Lonely the Boat

How strange it was to look out over the waters and see no land. When I was a small child and used to fish with my father, it was always comforting to see the land from our boat. Never did we go so far away from the shore that we could not mark our journey by land's view.

The first day after the rains stopped I went out alone and stood upon the top of the ark. What I saw was nothing . . . nothing but water. Below those waters were the now-silent voices of people who had mocked my building of such a strange vessel.

The voices were not silent when the waters began to rise. We all heard the screams of those who beat upon the great closed door. With animals as my audience I tried to explain to my children why I could not open it. Some of those voices belonged to friends with whom they had played only a few days earlier.

I walked away from their questions and their pleas. I walked among the animals, for they did not ask questions, and their clamor as I approached drowned out the screams from outside.

The harshness of God's voice still echoed in my ears along with the constant sound of hammering. My instructions had been detailed and clear. I was to build the boat a certain way with no questions asked. So when I asked about taking others on board, the certainty of the answer gave me great pause. The only answer I received was the constant thunder of ever-darkening clouds.

God seemed so close when it came to instructions but so very distant when it came to answering my questions. What kind of judgment must this be?

Our lonely journey lasted many days. I could see the impatience in the eyes of my family as well as the distance they had put between themselves and me. I had escaped God's waters only to be drowned in judgment by those I loved.

The day I brought the olive branch from the window, I saw the distance begin to close. Perhaps they realized that this was a new beginning that must be made together. The children rushed up toward the now-open window to see the sun upon the waters.

Near the end of the day I saw the bow in the clouds. I had always loved rainbows, but this one seemed to fill all of heaven, so it was not surprising to hear that voice of instruction again. This time the words came to me tenderly. Like the words of a parent who had felt the burden of punishing a child, they were words of hope and promise.

As God's words faded into the clouds, there was one last thunderclap laced with the sound of "never again." The rainbow seemed to cradle the words.

I gathered my family on the flat roof of the ark and pointed toward the rainbow. As I held my wife close to me and felt her gentle weeping, I looked out across the waters and imagined the ocean as tears from one who must be broken if he loved his children as I loved mine.

I tossed the olive branch into the waters and remembered how my father would hold me up on his shoulders when I was the scared child who had lost sight of the distant shore. He would point it out to me and laugh at my limited vision.

I lifted my youngest up onto my shoulders. I turned toward the now-fading rainbow and pointed out a distant shoreline. It was time to begin again. It was time to find out what this new promise really meant.

Talking When They Should Have Been Listening

What a sight it was! It was almost finished. Personally, I thought it was a great idea. So did most of my friends. We would build a tower so that we could see forever. We would pile together our skills and our bricks. It would be great.

The foundation of our building came long before the first brick was laid. Late-night discussions produced countless arguments about the gods. What were they like? Did they really exist? What kind of powers did they really possess? How much of what we had been told was mere words?

The majority opinion was that if the gods existed, their residence was just above our reach. Our tower was going to settle the argument. If we built it high enough, we could either converse with the gods or prove their unreality.

Some of our number urged caution. Stories from a distant land about the origin of our creation offered warnings of overstepping the bounds of being human. One of the elders abruptly left the room one night muttering something about when would we ever learn to stay out of places where we had no business going.

The point that won the day was when one of the younger would-be builders rose to his feet and said that if some god did not want us to build such a tower, then we would not possess the power to do it. The skills we possessed were proof that we should go forward with the planned tower to the heavens. "After all," he said, "were we not godlike?" Most agreed that it was time to check out our godlike status.

It was amazing how well we worked together on our tower. As the structure reached higher and higher toward the clouds, our sense of pride climbed with it. Surely this must be how the gods feel when they create something.

I pondered just what would be the limits of our creative ability. There seemed nothing we could not do if we set our minds to it. Others who came would see what we had done and conclude that surely this was the residence of a god.

Which one of us would assume the role of the god's

spokesman? Would we be able to agree on who would be in charge of the tower? It was an exciting thought.

Then came the storm. I was with the others when the lightning began striking all around us. Suddenly there were voices, voices that seemed to come from the thundering clouds . . . voices shouting words that I had never heard before.

My companions began repeating those words as if they were echoing the sounds. Each of us tried to speak to one another, but there was no understanding. I felt that I was speaking as I had always spoken, but those around me acted as if they didn't know what I was saying.

Had the thunder deafened us? What were these strange-sounding words coming from people who had the night before proclaimed our upcoming victory of labor?

We tried the next day to begin again. We were so close. The bricks waited, but the building blocks were gone. There was no longer any unity of purpose. We could not speak words that would be understood by one another.

Even though we could not communicate with words, we all knew the same reality. The gods who before had been distant powers to be overcome were now the conquerors. Our late-night conversations had been answered in the midst of that storm.

I wondered as I walked for the last time down the incomplete stairway to the heavens just which of the gods had done this thing. Was there now a god for every tongue that I had heard? Or could it be that there was only one god who must surely now be laughing at our inability to finish what we had started? Who was godlike now?

I shall now go with my own family, who still understands my words. We shall build new dwellings, but there will be no more towers to the sky. The old man who spoke that night was wise. We have no business going where we are not supposed to go. I wonder how many of my strange-speaking friends feel as I do.

Everybody's Grandfather

How long has it been since that afternoon when the wind spoke my name? Abram was a young man's name. The same hand that is responsible for the lines now drawn across my aged face is the hand that rewrote my life and my name.

I still do not know the name of the god who called my name. This is a god of promises, for the first words spoken to me were words of covenant. "If you will go," this god said, "I will make of you a great nation. Your many descendants will be called my children."

Why should I listen to these strange words muttered in the wind? A god I did not know was asking me to leave my home and go to a land across the mountains. Why listen?

I am not sure to this day why I did listen. Somewhere deep within my heart another voice whispered, "Go." The journey has been long and full of pain and laughter.

The laughter is dearer to my heart, for laughter was the name of the promise. This god promised me a child. I joined Sarah in her laughter, for we were all dried up. What kind of god could produce a crop in the desert? But a child did come, and Isaac had to be his name, for the wind said it must be so. Isaac . . . child of laughter.

Laughter still surrounded me that afternoon when the voice again spoke to me, telling me to take my child of laughter to a distant mountain and sacrifice him. The god of the wind became to me a demon that day. What kind of god asks for a child of promise?

But again the echo of my heart said, "Go." I still remember the look in my child's eyes as I bound him for the sacrifice. He did not question me, except with those eyes. He had heard me speak of the god with no name. He knew how mysterious the ways of this god were. Now the mystery was about to swallow up my child of promise.

As I raised the knife, the sounds of escape filled my ears. A ram whose horns had become entangled in the underbrush was struggling near the altar of sacrifice. My own child offered no struggle. Then the wind spoke to me again: "It is enough that you would do this thing. You may have your son whom I gave to you. Now he is fully your son and my son. Give to me the ram."

My vision grows dimmer each day now. These eyes have seen too much. The image of Ishmael being sent into the wilderness because he was "the other child" still haunts me. I no longer want to see such images. I want the burning destruction of Sodom and Gomorrah to fade from my sight. My bargaining with this god did no good that day.

Promises have been kept by this god of the wind who has no name. I have had to take many blind leaps of faith to walk the path of this promise. Always the wind spoke of trust.

Now my child of laughter inherits the land and my god. Be careful, my child. Where the wind will lead you is a mystery indeed.

God's Rascal

Egypt is not the land of promise. I question God's ways. Why are we so far from the land given to my father, Isaac, and to his father, Abraham?

I have always been one to question the God of my fathers. They named me Jacob because from my birth I refused to submit to the ways of God. Esau, my twin, was born first. The stories around the night fires recall that as Esau emerged from our mother's womb, I grabbed his heel so as to pull him back so that he would not be the firstborn. My name means "heel grabber."

Since God would not cooperate with my plan, I changed God's plan. Well, at least I thought I could change God's plan. Somehow this God of ours has a plan whose weaving I do not understand.

Rebekah, our mother, wanted me to have the blessing. She was my loving conspirator. Esau was wonderfully foolish. I had already tricked him out of his birthright for a bowl of stew. He was not worthy of being in charge of our father's plans. Surely God could see that. Why had I been born second? Birth order should not dictate ability. I changed all that . . . or tried to.

With Rebekah's assistance I fooled Isaac. He thought he was giving Esau the blessing. The rough animal skins stretched around my arms made him sure that he was granting burly Esau the blessing. Isaac was blind to his action because of his age. I was blind to what I was doing because of my youth and ambition.

I ran to tell my mother that our deception had been completed. As we embraced, the realization of what we had done surrounded us. What good was the blessing if I could not be truly the blessed one?

Esau's anger reached me before the sun set. I knew that I had to flee. I did not want to hurt my father yet again by having him blindly watch as my brother and I fought to see who would gain power.

God made my exile hard. The blessing continued to elude me even in my hiding. God's strange justice followed me as

I was tricked into working more than the agreed-upon number of years to gain Rachel as my bride. My seeds of deceit had grown into the fruit of constant frustration in a distant land.

In spite of the hardships, my herds multiplied in the new land. Life was good to me. Had I finally escaped the judgment of our God? I feared that the story was not over. Was not this the same God who had asked Abraham to offer my father Isaac as a sacrifice upon the mountain? What would this God require of me?

I found my answer as I attempted to sleep that night beside the river Jabbok. I had decided to return to my homeland and face my brother's wrath. The sweetness of all that I had gained in my new homeland could not destroy the bitter aftertaste in my life that came from the unfinished business I had with my family.

I knew that my brother had the legitimate right to take my life from me. The risk was worth the price. My new family thought I was brave to undertake this return home—brave and foolish. My deceit still covered my fear.

I drew away from my family as we came close to the time of reunion. I needed to be alone. That night under the stars sleep carried me to a place beyond the river.

I tried to awaken, but it seemed that it was not sleep that held me captive. There before my face was a being whose eyes held the fire of God. At first I tried to wrestle myself away from the one who seemed to be taking my life from me. My brother would be robbed of the pleasure of taking my life, for this angel of death seemed to know my name.

But I was Jacob, the great deceiver. No god-sent messenger was going to have the best of me. If I could not prevail, then at least this strange messenger would know with whom he wrestled.

Somehow in my struggle I seemed to get the upper hand. I still do not know from where the strength came for this battle. Perhaps I had been preparing for this struggle my whole life.

Then came the strange whisper surrounding my sweaty body: "Let me go." I feared letting go. Was it not better to die with the upper hand, if I must die? Ever wanting to gain blessing, I again asked for it. This time into the darkness of my struggle I screamed my response: "I will not let you go unless you bless me."

Then came the pain as if some arrow had pierced me. My hip became knotted in pain. Was this the first pain of my death? Had I asked too much? Whom did I now think I was deceiving? Was this one who held me not the one who made me what I am? Wanting to be first now surely would be my last request.

Into the midst of my pain came the reply, "What is your name?" I knew that this question was aimed not at gaining information but at forcing me to learn something. My name needed to be spoken into the struggle, for its meaning needed to be exposed.

Was this God's strange humor? Was I to be naked in my shame? Was I to be reminded yet again that I did not deserve a blessing?

Then the voice in the midst of the struggle announced, "Your name shall no longer be Jacob, but Israel, for you have struggled with God and prevailed."

When I woke, the dream faded, but the pain in my side remained. I screamed into the early morning mist, "What is your name?" From within me came the reply, "You need not know my name; remember your name."

Was this some night vision, or was it God? All I know is that even in my old age I walk with a limp. Esau surprised all by forgiving me and granting me the blessing I had always wanted in the very moment I had ceased seeking it. My twelve sons now are reminders of God's strange promise to me. I will not escape the angel of death this time. Here in Egypt I am still asking questions of this mysterious God. My youngest son, Joseph, himself the victim of deception by the seeds of my own planting, now cares for us. Having been sold into slavery by jealous brothers who tried to fool me with tales of his death, Joseph now takes us back with forgiveness and blessing.

But why are we in Egypt? Why so far away from the land of promise? What thread of mystery has our God woven into the tapestry this time?

I do not trust these Egyptians. It takes a deceiver's heart

to recognize those who would deceive. Somehow I feel our
future here is one of trouble. The wrestling match is over, but
I continue my struggle with the ways of God. "One who
struggles with God and prevails. . . ." I wonder.

The Freedom Dance

Unless you have experienced the bitterness of captivity, you cannot imagine how sweet freedom tastes. Beside those waters of deliverance I danced. No permission was asked, though our custom required such. I did not wait upon some man to gesture for me to sing the song in my heart. There on the edge of the waiting wilderness I simply allowed my heart its freedom.

> Sing to the Lord, for he has triumphed
>   gloriously;
> horse and rider he has thrown
>   into the sea.

Those were the words that I sang over and over again. Other women joined me in reckless abandon. The sound of the timbrels still echoes in my memory.

I too had doubted Moses. Our brother Aaron told me to quiet my tongue when I joined in the murmuring of the people as we stood helpless beside the sea. Why had Moses led us into the desert only to die at the hands of Pharaoh's anger? Was our freedom to be only a preparation for our death in the wilderness?

The angel of death had unbound Pharaoh's heart, but the price had been his firstborn. No god was going to tell the king what to do. On that terrible, yet wonderful night of deliverance the only voice Pharaoh could hear was the desperate pleading of his queen to do something to save the life of her child. The stone gods of Egypt listened and gave the only response they could. Silence.

Pharaoh felt the power of our God. The loss of his heir did what no plague could do. In his grief he let us go, but as his tears dried, his anger welled up within him.

As we stood watching the dust of Pharaoh's chariots in the distance, we knew that the slavery we would face back in Egypt would be unbearable. To know freedom for such a short time was a cruel tease. Why was God doing this?

I felt for Moses even as I spoke ill of him. My faith was buried beneath my fear. He walked away from our shallow believing and faced the sea alone. Was he going to throw himself into the waves? The waters of the sea had to be more welcoming than the people whose love for him was like a morning dew that fades with the sun.

"O Moses," I thought, "you should have stayed in that land of exile far away tending sheep, for the sheep you now lead follow not your way unless all is well." The demands upon this one man were far too many.

I walked up behind Moses to confess my own doubt but also to assure him of my love for him. Perhaps he could bargain with Pharaoh's soldiers and avoid the massacre that awaited in those distant clouds of dust and hatred.

He seemed to be talking to the sea. My poor brother could find no one to listen, so he was casting his words upon the waters.

Suddenly he turned toward us. He saw me reach up to him, and he smiled. What kind of madness had possessed him? Speaking with our God had finally broken him.

He lifted his hands to the people and shouted, "Stand ready, O children, and watch the salvation of your God. Have faith."

Turning toward the sea, he lifted his staff. The winds blew the sand so that we had to cover our eyes. As we slowly walked toward Moses, what was happening became clear. The waters were being pushed about as if it was the mud in the pits of Egypt being stirred in preparation for the making of bricks, the bricks of our hated captivity.

There before us was a path through the waters. For the first time in many days Moses' flock was silent. What could be said in the face of a God who tames the sea?

We made our way through the waters, adding to them only the tears of our joy. As Pharaoh's soldiers attempted to follow this strange path, Moses again raised his hands, and the winds shifted. The waters surrounded the chariots. There was no escape. Now our captors were captive, enslaved by the watery chains of a God of surprises.

I danced because I had to dance. I danced to offer God my little faith, which had been held captive by my doubt. I broke my chains of fear with my joyous movement.

Now we face a long journey. Where will this God of

surprises lead us? I shall continue to sing into the wind. I will lead others in the dance of the desert.

On long, dry days when my people cannot remember the songs of their hearts, I will sing the songs for them. I shall remember the waters of my own deliverance. I shall teach the songs to our children. The songs shall not die, though many of us may perish on this journey.

O God of paths in the sea, teach me more songs. I am your daughter of struggling faith, but I know how to dance. Lead me, and I will lead others in your dance of deliverance.

The Other Woman

Some say that I was the victim, that I had no choice, but I knew what I was doing. To be asked to come to his chambers awoke my sleeping heart. Yes, I loved Uriah as a wife should love her husband. I had been faithful to him until that afternoon on which an invitation came to my hungry heart. The duty of my love for my husband had hollowed a place within my soul.

I walked toward David's palace holding that vacancy within me. I had seen my king only from a distance. He was more than a king. I had noticed him look my way on one of those celebration days as he marched before his soldiers. I should have been proudly looking toward my own soldier, who had gained a reputation as being a noble fighter. Uriah's feats had established him as one of David's finest. Why then was I that day looking at David and not at my soldier-husband?

Only in my fantasy did I allow my dreams to take me to his chambers. Uriah did love me, but he loved his duty first. He was in love with being a soldier. His first loves were country and king. I was only part of his loving, and so it was that a portion of me would find itself longing for David's chambers.

I imagined myself dreaming when my king lay with me that first night. As his body became part of mine, the empty place in my soul was filled. Only a few hours earlier he had sent away the one who had come to escort me to his chambers. As David's eyes met mine, we said nothing to each other.

I knew he could have any woman he wanted, but we both knew he was not supposed to have me. The God who had chosen him to be king did not allow it even if the powers of a king made it possible.

When he finally spoke, it was not the authoritarian voice I had so often heard as he addressed the people. His words were soft and gentle. He had watched me from his balcony as I bathed. He had watched me other times. My heart soared even as it sank deep within my chest, for I knew in that moment that we were both lost to our feelings.

78

As he held me, I felt the embrace not of a king but of a playful boy who had written songs and poems. He was the tender shepherd who had cared for so many wounded, lost sheep. I was willing to be lost with him.

I gave myself to him as I had never done with Uriah. There was no trying. There was simply giving.

His embrace left me empty and full. How could such a strong man make love so tenderly? The mystery of his craft held me as I was shaped by his loving of me.

We held each other in silence after the loving. Outside that room my husband and David's servant was faithfully safeguarding the kingdom. Both David and I knew that we had stepped over a narrow fence that had been placed between us by a God who knew no compromise. Even so, there was joy.

I went to David as often as he would send for me. It was no surprise when I became filled with life. Now there could be no hiding our secret pleasure. Uriah had not been with me. He had been away serving his king and my lover.

David tried in every way he could to cover our sin. He brought Uriah back from the front line to give him the opportunity to lie with me. But David did not know my Uriah. He would take no pleasure with me while his fellow companions were sleeping miles away from their wives and families.

Even when David filled him with wine and sent him to me, Uriah slept outside the door. Those who witnessed my husband's faithfulness marveled at his honor.

My poor king was torn in two. He had not wanted Uriah to be with me, yet he knew that he had to do something to conceal our love. When he saw that his deception would not work, he conspired to have Uriah placed in the heart of battle, hoping that the enemy would do what a king could not do.

The plan worked. Uriah became a noble hero in his death. I became an available widow.

We were both fools. We hid nothing from anyone. We hid behind a crown, but the crown was not big enough to conceal our sin. The king made the law, but it was our God who made the king.

Did we think God would forget? Nathan, the ever-present prophet, had to remind the king that God was not some old man whose memory had failed. When Nathan pointed his staff at David with words of judgment, he announced that not only would we be judged but my child would die. The price of our sin was growing.

I held David in my arms as he wept. I was numb. He had begged God to take his life instead of the child's. It was his sin, not the child's. But God would have none of it. The shepherd boy had forgotten how to sing. His tears poured down my breast as we watched our child die.

I wept for my king. I wept for my child. I wept for our sin. I wept because, in spite of our sin and all the wrong we had done, I still loved my shepherd king.

My broken-hearted king was reminded by God that the story was not over. There was more that needed doing. Punishment did not mean that God had forgotten that David was "his beloved." That did not change. This God knew the heart of the shepherd better than I. The people needed the shepherd.

Life went on. I conceived again. His name is Solomon. He is a beautiful child. My king and I wept again as we held Solomon up before the altar and dedicated him to God. How amazing is our God in the ways he uses broken people to accomplish his will.

Some still look at me as the "other woman," but I am willing to be what they need me to be. I have paid dearly for my love. I cannot bring back my child who was conceived in the passion of my lost heart, but neither will I let go of the king who becomes a little boy in my arms.

David is near to God's heart. I know that. His people know that. God understands David's forgetting even though he does not overlook it. I share something with God, for only we know the real David. He is the strong leader who is really a little boy who writes verse on long, lonely nights. He is the shepherd whose craftiness and skill gained him more than he could handle.

He is the lonely shepherd who got lost one afternoon while walking on his balcony. O David, how I love you. Thank you, O God, for somehow loving my shepherd king even more than I love him.

Hide and Seek

His mantle is heavy. Many times I have wanted to cast it aside. Being God's prophet is lonely. This God keeps asking me to do things that seem beyond my abilities. My love for the people and the country was known by God. It is hard to speak words of judgment. Often I have wanted to soften the harshness of God's words, but they are like fire in my bones. This mantle seems some days more like a curse.

I find myself the go-between for a God who will not speak directly to the people. Being willing to be used means being liable to be used up. How many times I have wanted to scream back at him to do his own talking, but I knew it would do no good. God's persistence seems deeper than even his love. There is no escaping.

When I was hungry, he fed me. Even the ravens knew that I was his prophet. The poor widow whose house I was led to had no use for a prophet. What she needed was bread for her family. Words were no substitute for food.

I did not blame her for kicking dust over my feet when I assured her that God would provide enough food for all of us. She had grown tired of promises. Her will to believe had grown empty along with her storehouse.

So it was that when the meal in the bowl was replenished each evening after she used it up, she believed me to be some kind of god. I assured her that I had less understanding of how God did this than she. I simply did what God asked me to do.

I can be bold, or at least I can act bold. That day on Mount Carmel when I challenged the prophets of Baal showed how foolish for God I could be. I had no idea what would really happen. I again risked all for God and watched his power fall from heaven.

What we all beheld that day was an awesome display of God's jealousy. Not only did the fire from heaven consume the sacrifice, but God's vengeance claimed the lives of those poor fools who worshiped their blocks of wood. God had no room for compromise that cloudy afternoon.

While the fire was still smoldering, a chilly fear surrounded me. What had I done? The victory would be shortlived, for Jezebel would have the last word. She would send her bloodthirsty hounds after me. I would be the next sacrifice. I slipped into the night and journeyed to a nearby cave. I was afraid—afraid both that Jezebel would find me and that God would find me. Both wanted my life.

God teased me. At first there was the tearing of the wind. The earth shook, and I thought he would consume me as he had consumed that sacrifice on the mountain. My cave of hiding would become my tomb. I knew firsthand the power of this God.

I screamed into the darkness, "Is that you, my God?" There was no reply. After the quiet came the lightning. The evening sky was filled with the thunder and brightness of his wrath. All around the entrance to the cave the burning, reaching fingers of his fire set the underbrush aflame.

Which of his shows of power would take my life? Then came the rain. It was a gentle rain, and again I saw smoldering fires. The breeze touched my face as I stood looking out over his power. I whispered my plea: "Are you there, God?"

This time there was only quiet. In the midst of the breeze I heard his voice almost like the soft song of a bird late in the evening, "What are you doing here, Elijah?"

I issued forth my complaint. I told him I was afraid. I offered my excuses for hiding. As if he did not know what I felt, I made sure he knew. I was tired of being his instrument.

What did he do? Nothing. As if I had not said one word, he began telling me what I was to do next. Amazingly the gentle breeze cradled me. The earthquake, wind, and fire were but memories while I felt the strange power of his gentleness for the first time. Suddenly I was a child again being held by my mother. Nursed by the sustaining breeze, I felt mystical courage flowing in my bent frame.

There is no hiding place. I will go again for him. I never know how he will appear, for now his power has reached me in the shaking earth and in the stillness of the breeze.

God's Foolish Lover

My father no longer claimed me. When I approached my brothers, they would turn and walk away. Those who used to be friends either whispered their disgust or laughed openly at my foolishness. Kindness led some to believe that I had lost my mind, while others simply thought that I was a man desperate for a woman's body.

Her eyes first met mine at the well. Her face was drawn, but her look was somehow inviting. To how many men had she offered herself?

I asked her if she would come to my house. She smiled and responded that she would go anywhere if the price was right. What price had she paid in the past to offer herself now in this way?

She followed behind me as was the custom. I told her that I had been watching her from a distance for days. She laughed and asked me if I had been shopping. She became suddenly quiet when I told her that I was a prophet and that God had told me to go down to the place where the harlots gathered so that I might choose a wife.

From anger or the remaining pride still buried within her came her response: "I can be purchased for an evening but not for a lifetime." I assured her that I wanted to release her from the bondage of selling herself. She pulled herself away from me and told me that she was what she was.

I counted out the expected fee and handed it to her. She asked me how I wanted it. Looking down at the floor, I told her she was free to go. "You must be some kind of fool," she blurted before she walked out.

After she left, I fell on the floor and wept. I begged God to leave me alone. Why had he asked me to prostitute myself for his strange ways? His demanding voice had told me to go to the well and draw forth a woman.

The next afternoon his voice returned: "Go find out her name." I protested. Why a harlot? Did God not realize what a mockery this was?

It was then that his words of judgment pressed upon me like a weight: "Do you not see, Hosea? My people have betrayed my love for them. They have sold themselves to other lovers. I want them to see what they have done. If they see that I still love them after their whoring ways, perhaps they will turn and take me as their only lover."

"But my God," I pleaded, "look at the personal price I must pay to be your parable." Silence was my answer. I had no choice but to listen to this strange request. I was God's prophet in a day when people had grown tired of hearing the word of the Lord. Perhaps if the people could see something, they would again hear.

I went to that place near the well every afternoon. Each day she would follow me to my house. I never took her flesh. I tried to touch her with my words. She seemed untouchable except in the way she was used to being touched.

On one of my "purchased" nights she turned from the window through which she had been staring and spoke words that left my heart both full and empty: "I will marry you, but you must understand that I do not know if there is loyalty within me. I have never known the kind of compassion you now offer me. The only love I know is the kind I try to give those who purchase it. This god of yours is persistent. I will try this new kind of love."

Gomer did try. She bore me children. God told me that the children must be named so that the people who watched our strange marriage would be certain that a clear message was being given to the people through our children. God was speaking in and through our relationship.

Our children's names were names of judgment. Jezreel was our first, meaning that God would remember the sins of the past. God had not been sleeping, though the people thought he had.

Gomer then bore me a daughter. When God told me what to name her, I wept. She was to be called "Not Pitied."

Not sparing my own broken heart, our next son was named "Not My People." Gomer must have felt that she was again being purchased and used. God's price was high.

Gomer began to be open with her adultery after the birth of our last son. She told me that she was tired of being some kind of puppet for God and me. She would drink wine in the afternoon and go down to her old station by the well in the evening.

One of the evenings she did not return. I felt a sense of relief. I was tired of her unfaithfulness. I had grown weary of God's words about steadfast love. I was broken from being God's harlot.

I announced the words of judgment to the people. I told them that they had been the harlot. I screamed at the city gate that God would surely punish the nation's adulterous life because the people had given their love to other gods. Some people listened, but most thought that I either was mad or was simply trying to make some sense out of my own contemptible relationship.

Deep into the night, on one of those many evenings when sleep was no companion for me, God's word returned. One of my children was crying in the night. I comforted her with an embrace. As I returned to my bed, feeling pity for my own condition, God spoke into the night.

As I listened, I wondered if this God would ever make up his mind. He seemed to be confused about his love for the people. Then I thought of my feelings toward Gomer and my own children. I wrote what I heard him say:

> When Israel was a child, I loved him,
>   and out of Egypt I called my son.
> The more I called them,
>   the more they went from me . . .
> Yet it was I who taught my children to walk,
>   I took them up into my arms;
>   but they did not know that I healed them.
> I led them with cords of compassion,
>   with bonds of love. . . .

Then my room became filled with what seemed like a burning fire, as he continued:

> . . . but they refused to turn to me
> The sword shall rage against their cities. . . .
> My people are bent on turning away
>   from me;

> So they are appointed to the yoke,
> and none shall remove it. . . .

Then there was silence . . . silence as when a parent is trying to decide what to do with a wayward child. I could almost hear weeping.

> How can I give you up . . .
> How can I hand you over?
> My heart recoils within me, my compassion
> grows warm and tender.
> I will not destroy you, my child,
> for I am God and not man.

Who is this God who struggles so with his love for us? I knew the time of punishment was coming. God would not be mocked. But in these words of a parent for his children, I felt God's heart break.

This was the God who led me to the harlots' place by the well. This was the God who had taught me to love even the one who was unfaithful to me. This was a God whose love seemed bigger than our sin.

O God, I know what I must do now. You do not need to speak into the night. I know . . . I know. I must go find Gomer.

The Unexpectant Mother

Please answer the door. O God, please let him answer the door. My pain is becoming unbearable. It is late. The life within me is wanting birth. Joseph, speak quickly to this strange face and tell him of our need. You need not tell him everything, for he will not believe such a story. I am barely able to believe it myself. Just tell him of our plight and ask him for a room.

The months have passed quickly since that afternoon when my life was broken open by a voice through my window. The light was blinding, and the voice was one speaking of the impossible. Perhaps I should not have responded to such a vision, but my fear or my innocence shoved me toward the light.

I had not known the touch of a man. How could I now give what I had not received? My ancestor Jacob had wrestled with his angel. As he limped away from his place of struggle, his life and his name were forever changed. I questioned my angel, for the change that was to come over me was beyond any thought. How could this be?

The voice gave me the strange promise of new life within me. My father had taught me never to question God, but my father had never had to hold up under the weight of being the fulfillment of prophecy.

I told this voice within the light that I was simply Mary, no more and no less. The reply was a strange assurance that I was enough for God.

My Joseph turned away from me when he first heard my news. I could not blame him. I had struggled to believe the words myself. I would awake in the morning and lie in my bed trying to remember if it all had been a dream.

When Joseph came back later, he found me weeping. God's word had left me so very alone. I was to hold hope for the world, but who would hold hope for me? I tried to be strong, but can anyone stand under such a heavy promise?

I could not look into Joseph's face. I did not want to see again his disappointment. He reached down to me. As I looked into his eyes, I quickly saw that he too had been crying. O Joseph, how I had hurt you.

But his words were no longer full of doubt and disappointment. He told me that he now understood. Tell me then of understanding, Joseph, for my acceptance has surpassed my understanding. I do not know if I will ever understand.

Joseph assured me that he would stand with me and our son. How did he know it would be a son? Had God's afternoon light blinded him too? Had he been overshadowed with the same mystery that had surrounded me?

It mattered not from where he had gained such faith. All that mattered was that I was no longer alone with my promise.

Even when I shared the news with Elizabeth, I did it with hesitation. Her smile of recognition preceded her announcement to me of life stirring within her.

What was God doing? So many deserts blooming. Had God unleashed the power of heaven? How many more impossible things would I encounter before God's promise broke forth from my womb?

But what are these words you now speak to me, Joseph—words about "no room"?

O Joseph, there must be room for my pain. Did you tell him of the coming child? Does he not care?

O Joseph, tell him of angels, and of old women giving birth, and of prophecies being fulfilled in our very midst. Tell him anything, Joseph, for lies will make more sense this night than the truth.

Where are you taking me, Joseph? What is this you whisper to me with such tones of understanding? O strong interpreter of angels' voices, how can you be leading me to a stable? Joseph, call out to our angel and protest this message of "no room." Surely this cannot be how God wants the birth to happen.

But my pain now blurs the questions. Lay me anywhere, Joseph. The animals seem not to mind. Perhaps they have as much understanding as anyone on this still night. The child is near. I am afraid. Where is my angel? Hold me, Joseph. Hold me.

Just a Local Rabbi

At first there was nothing particularly special about him. He was pensive and reserved. He would come to me with other boys from the village for weekly instruction. Our history and our Scriptures are the only thing that the Romans could not take from us.

I wanted my students to learn to love the Law and the Prophets, not just memorize them. The words needed to be planted in their young hearts, not shelved in the far corners of their minds. As I taught them, I never knew which of them was really learning to love these sacred words from our past. Some were simply being obedient children.

But as for him, there was never a doubt. At first he did not speak much except when called on. He drank in my words like a pilgrim drinking water after a long journey. In his eyes was an eagerness seldom seen on the face of one so young.

Many of my former students had been bright. Oftentimes boys would compete with each other as if in an athletic contest. But this son of Mary and Joseph seemed not just to be memorizing texts. When he spoke the words of our ancient writings they took on new life. He spoke them as if they were words from a letter he had received from a loving relative.

I was the only one who was not surprised when Jesus' family could not find him that year after the festival. I remember trying to comfort Mary when she discovered that he was not with other relatives on the trip home from Jerusalem. I reminded her that Jesus was now a "man" according to our religion. She looked at me as only a mother can, and I knew my words were empty. I was the local rabbi. She was his mother.

I journeyed back to the city with Mary and Joseph to look for Jesus. They wanted first to go to the home where they had stayed during the festival days. I grabbed Mary's hand and looked into her frantic eyes. I suggested that I knew where he might be.

As I walked up the Temple steps, I saw one of my friends, the rabbi in Capernaum. He was coming down the steps from the courtyard. I motioned to him to come my way so that I could ask him if he had seen our lost young man.

Before I could offer even a word of greeting, he laughed and placed his hand upon my shoulder. The words he spoke made my heart smile: "There is a young lad sitting over there on one of the Temple porches who is baffling the priests and elders. He speaks words from Scripture as if he is an actor who has memorized all the lines for a drama. I have never heard words spoken with such passion, especially from someone so young. He handles even the hard questions tossed to him by the priests as if he had been trained to do so. I would like to meet his teacher."

I know that pride is a sin, but then rabbis know sin first-hand. Pride swelled up within me as I smiled and said, "Could it be that his name is Jesus?"

"Yes it is. Why?"

"He is one of mine . . ."

I walked away before the warm embarrassment I felt became so obvious. As I came up behind Joseph and Mary, I could tell that the moneychangers cared little about their questions. There was nothing in it for them.

I spoke gently to Mary. "I think I have found him." If I could have captured the look in her eyes at that moment, I would never again have to fill my lamps with oil. I could simply pour the power of that look into my lamps, and there would be light in the room.

We walked, almost ran, to one of the porches next to the main entrance of the Temple. A large group of men was gathered around. From where I stood, the reason for their assembly could not be seen, but I knew what it was.

Mary did not need to be told that she could not go up those steps. She knew of our law. Women, even frightened mothers, could not go into this part of the Temple.

I asked Joseph to stay with her and assured her that I would go to see if my suspicion was correct. As I made my way through the crowd, I could see Jesus motioning with his hands; he was responding to a question about one of the prophecies from Isaiah.

Some of the older men were laughing with a kind of quiet respect. I could tell that they were captivated by his response.

I spoke but one word: "Jesus." He looked my way and immediately stood. "Rabbi, have you come for me?"

The elders looked my way. Never have I been filled with such pride. Jesus walked up beside me, turned back to the wide-eyed priests who were standing on the upper steps, made a slight bow of respect, and picked up the stride of my steps.

As we made our way toward a waiting mother and father, Mary eagerly started to step into the area forbidden to her. Joseph kindly restrained her. Jesus put out his arms, and Mary pulled him into her excited reach. I was unable to walk away, even though I knew that this should be a private moment between them. Through her tears Mary lovingly chastised her son, recounting her worry for him.

Jesus looked almost stunned as if she should have known where he had been. He tilted his head slightly and said, "Mother, did you not know that I would be about my father's business?"

I looked up at Joseph to see if he would respond. Joseph was a carpenter. What kind of craft could his son be practicing on the Temple steps?

Joseph made no response; nor was there any surprise on his face. He simply said, "Let's go home."

All of this happened years ago. Jesus finished his instruction and became just another one of the young men of the village. The years passed like sands sifting in the desert wind. He came to synagogue, but never again did he speak anything out of the ordinary. That is, until the other day.

Word spread that he had left Nazareth. Rumors came back, strange rumors of his teaching in other synagogues. Why had he not taught in his own?

Then last Sabbath as I was preparing to ask someone to read from the text of the day, I looked up and saw him enter the room. I could hear the whispers of the other men, and I knew what I must do. I held up the scroll for him. He stood and read the words:

> The Spirit of the Lord is upon me,
> because he has anointed me to preach good news
> to the poor.
> He has sent me to proclaim release to the captives
> and recovering of sight to the blind,

to set at liberty those who are oppressed,
to proclaim the acceptable year of the Lord.

His voice was as it had been on that day in the Temple. He did not appear to be simply reading from the scroll; rather, he spoke the words as if he had written them himself.

Then he sat down. The room was exceptionally quiet. Every man knew that something special had just happened even though the words were familiar ones.

Then Jesus spoke words that troubled the waters. Looking out the window as if he was far away from us he said, "Today this scripture has been fulfilled in your hearing."

The room suddenly erupted with comment. I heard one elder say, "Is this not Joseph's son?" Some started questioning each other about what this meant.

Then Jesus talked about a prophet's not being understood in his own land. He told the story of Elijah and the widow. He spoke sternly of how the people of Israel seemed unable to listen to the words that God continually sent to them.

I could see the indignation filling the room. I wanted to take Jesus' hand as I had done that day on the Temple steps and lead him away from a sea of words that might drown him.

The indignation turned suddenly to anger. My people are easily enraged when someone plays with their hopes. This local boy had forgotten his place. To be a good teacher was one thing. To suddenly claim to be a prophet . . . well, that was something else.

Some pushed him out the door of the synagogue. Others completely lost their senses and wanted to cast him off a nearby cliff. One man, who had studied next to Jesus as a lad, quoted some Scripture to justify ridding the village of false prophets. I thought to myself, "You never seemed interested enough in the Scriptures to care, and now you quote them to do harm to one of your own."

I raised my hand. I did not need to speak a word. We are a rebellious people, but in our trampled culture we still have respect for local rabbis. The crowd, which had now become a mob, quieted. Jesus looked over to me as he had so many other times.

I spoke painful words to him, but they were words that

needed to be spoken: "My child, perhaps you should leave now."

He looked into my eyes with a measure of kindness that I have never seen in human eyes. He touched my sleeve with his hand and walked out into the arid afternoon.

Be careful, O special student of mine. Our people may not be ready for your kind of wisdom.

The One Who Remembered

Between Samaria and Galilee is where they put us. Since we were the garbage of life, no country wanted us. This place was distant from life.

I was not always garbage. My childhood was fairly normal. When I was not learning my father's trade, I played on the hills outside our village. Then it happened. One of the other boys noticed the small white place on my arm. He ran away screaming, "Unclean, unclean."

Laughter was my first response. This was not the first time one of us had played a cruel joke on the other. Leprosy, however, was no joking matter.

Looking down at my arm, I did notice that in the afternoon light there was more than one patch of discolored skin. I touched my finger to one of the places, and fear crept over me. There was no feeling in the colorless area.

That evening I showed my arm to my mother. She wept. The next morning before sunrise my father awakened me. There were but a few words spoken, and they were said so that I could not hear.

The village rabbi was waiting for us when my father and I arrived at his house. He looked at my arm, whispered something to my father, and quickly walked back inside his house. When we arrived back home, the sun was just coming up. My father picked up a blanket that had been tied up to form a kind of pack.

"We must go now, my son. If we do not take you from the village, you will be stoned." I asked if I could kiss my still-sleeping mother. The tone of his voice frightened me. "Don't touch your mother."

As we walked away from the village, I thought of the conversations we had had about lepers. Lepers simply disappeared. One of the boys said they were taken to a place in the desert and thrown off a cliff. I remember the laughter we had shared. How could we have laughed?

My father said nothing to me as we walked a day's journey. We came to a path leading down into a valley. My father turned to me. I looked up at him. He had been crying. Is this why he had not ever turned my way while we walked? I had never seen my father cry. He spoke. "My son, I am sorry. These people will care for you. If you stayed at home, not only would you be stoned, it would put our whole family at the mercy of the people. We will pray for you. I'm sorry. Goodbye."

That was the last time I saw my father. I learned basic survival in the colony. The customary segregation of Samaritan and Jew was abolished in this valley of lepers. Our disease had done what no law or religion could do. We were together in our need.

I was not as ill as many. Death was commonplace here. Often some of our number would venture out to beg for food as travelers passed by. Usually something was given to us out of both pity and recognition of the need to keep us away from the rest of life.

One day I was convinced to join a small group outside the entrance. They had told me that rumors of a healer coming our way were spreading throughout the colony. Caravans had spoken of a man who possessed a special power from God. I had little use for a God who allowed people to become garbage. I went with my companions that day out of curiosity more than hope.

A small group of people came our way. One man among them seemed to be speaking as they walked. One of our number said, "His name is Jesus." They began shouting, "Jesus, have mercy on us." I said nothing. I was not going to beg for anything, even healing.

"Shout, you fool," my bandaged friend scolded. I said nothing.

I looked up. The sun was immediately behind the solitary figure who had come over to us. Our crowd backed away. We knew the law. We were not to approach any person. But this man came up to us.

He raised his hand as if to give us a blessing. Yet another religious type praying some unanswered prayer for our plight. I had no use for his blessing.

He walked away toward the small group that accompanied him. They were not about to come as close to us as he had. He turned to us and said, "Go show yourselves to a priest." Then he was gone.

A priest had to confirm that a person was no longer a leper. It seldom happened. Why should we waste a trip only to be disappointed by some wandering healer's strange words? As some of our band started walking away from the colony, I called out, "Where do you think you are going? Do you believe anything has really happened to you? I still see lepers with bandages. What priest will even look at us?"

Then it happened. I felt suddenly warm, almost hot. I looked over to one of our number and saw that his face was no longer discolored. He tore off his bandages. His skin was full of the color of life. I slowly untied the bandage around my arm. I could feel the underneath part of my arm. I had not felt anything in that part of my arm for years.

Everyone began leaping for joy. "Let's go, let's go. Now we really have something to show a priest."

I stopped. "What about this Jesus? Where did he go? We need to find him and bow before him. Who is he?"

"No . . . we must go to a priest. Otherwise no one will believe we are truly healed. You know the law."

They were quickly gone. I ran toward where this Jesus had been. I looked to the far horizon. I could barely see the outline of his small group.

I ran toward him. His companions ran away. Only he turned. I threw myself at his feet. Then he did it. He touched me. I drew back. I had not been touched in years.

I looked up into his face and through my tears managed to say, "Thank you, oh, thank you." He gently lifted my head toward him. "Where are the others?

He turned toward his companions, who appeared terrified at what he had just done. No one touched lepers.

He said, more to them than to me, "Look who has come to say thank you . . . a Samaritan."

Had he recognized my accent? I had not thought of myself as a Samaritan for years. I was simply a leper. And now this man recognized this difference that had once mattered so much. Was I again to be an outcast for my beliefs? What beliefs? What did I believe? It had been so long.

This Jesus must have been a Jew. A Jew who cared. All I knew was that he must be one who was very close to God.

Can such a power not overcome the differences between Jew and Samaritan?

As he walked away, he turned to me and said, "Go, my friend. Your faith has made you well."

What little faith I had. He must be able to use even the smallest faith to work his miracles. He touched me. My life will never be the same. He touched me.

The Cross Bearer

Why me? I was simply one of the crowd. It would have been reasonable to pick one of his followers or at least someone who was sympathetic to his cause. I was but an onlooker.

To be drawn into such a scene was frightening, to say the least. I had heard of Roman crucifixions. The cruelty of such a death was known throughout the region. As I picked up the heavy beam of his cross, my first thought was to wonder if there would be another cross for me. I knew there was no particular reason that the guards had selected me, so I figured it would be of little significance to them to add one more to the count of those who were to be put to death that afternoon.

I had done nothing to deserve this, but then from what I knew, this Jesus had done nothing to earn this mockery either. The guard who picked me out of the crowd had a whip in his hand, and I knew it was not for some animal. It was for those who disobeyed. Most of these soldiers did not want to be in this "god-forsaken country," as they put it. They often took out their frustration on the people.

Carrying the heavy wood, I wondered how he had even managed to carry it as far as he had. It was obvious that he had been beaten. Who knows how long he had been denied food and water? Around his head was some kind of crown made out of thorns. Down his face were lines of dried blood. One of his eyes was swollen shut from the punishment he had received.

I had heard his name before. That is why I was even as close to the procession as I was. This misguided prophet had somehow influenced my two sons, Alexander and Rufus. They had told me of his revolutionary words.

We were not Jews. Why would they want to listen to a Jew from Nazareth?

My sons told me of his proclamation that the kingdom of God was open to all, not just the Jews. I did not care to whom this kingdom was open. I had encountered enough Jews to know that I wanted nothing to do with their god.

Their god lived in a temple in Jerusalem and had dictated rigid rules for the people to follow. Some of those rules kept "unclean" people like me at a distance. The Jews would have nothing to do with my business because I was both a foreigner and "unclean."

I told my children to forget the words of this Jewish prophet. I trusted none of his people or their ideas. How had my sons been taken in so easily?

They kept going to the places he was to speak. They started talking to me about loving enemies and turning the other cheek when struck. I told them such idle talk was both ridiculous and dangerous.

When they told me he could heal people and that some had told of a person being raised from death, I knew that trouble was ahead for this man and his followers. Rome would not have one of the Jews gain such popularity with the people.

My boys were young and naive. The windows of their lives were left open for any strange breeze to blow in. I told them to stay away from this Jesus. They seemed not to care. It was as if this strange itinerant preacher had cast a spell over them.

So it was that when I went to Jerusalem for the festival days in order to conduct some business, I had decided to check out this Jesus. Surely a Jewish leader would make an appearance during the high and holy days. I would see for myself what was so captivating about this man.

I inquired about him and was told that he was on trial for his life. I suddenly feared for my boys. Were they close enough to him to have been arrested? What was the charge? No one seemed to be sure.

I was told that he was being held in the Praetorium. As I approached the walled entrance, I heard cries from a crowd of people. Their tone was angry and unruly. The only distinct message I could hear was the repetition of the cry, "Crucify him." What poor fool was being convicted by such a crowd?

From my place in the back of the mass of people I could see what looked to be a Roman official. He had a basin in front of him, and he was washing his hands. What strange custom had I walked in on?

It was then that the crowd became a kind of mob. I made

my way down the street behind the Praetorium. A group of people already lined the street. I asked why they were there.

"He will be coming this way. We want to see if he will be able to carry his cross. We have bets on how far he will make it."

"Who is being crucified?"

"Some character named Jesus. He claims to be king of the Jews. Well, this king is going to have a short reign."

"Is he a king?"

"For God's sake, man, we don't care. You see what happens to any other king beside Herod or Pilate, don't you?"

I should have left then and tried to find my boys, but I wanted to see this Jesus. I wanted to see the man who was going to be crucified and who had captured the minds of my sons.

I walked farther down the road. Those who were betting on his life made strange company. I stood beside a group of women. I was surprised to see them in such a place. They were talking softly to each other. I knew they were not supposed to talk to me in public, but I ventured a question of them: "Do you know this man, Jesus?"

At first they looked away from me. I should not have spoken my next words. They were risky.

"My two sons are sort of followers of this Jesus. I am concerned for their safety. Please. Do you know anything about what is happening?"

One of the women then turned to me. I could tell that she had been crying.

"Do not fear for your sons. No other follower of his is dying today. His followers are all in hiding. My son dies alone."

This Jesus was her son! My wife had died four years earlier. I felt for this poor woman who must now watch her boy carry a cross to his place of death. I wanted to ask her what he had done to merit such action, but I knew that the question was inappropriate for such a moment. Besides, suddenly it no longer mattered what he had done. If my children thought something of this man, I sensed that he was dying because someone must fear his kind of foolishness.

Two other poor souls walked in front of Jesus as they made their way toward the place where we were standing. They too had cross beams roped to their arms. The wooden beam carried by Jesus was not strapped on. I gently asked his mother, "Is that last one your son?"

"Yes, that is him. . . . O my God, that is him."

I figured it must be so, for I had heard one of the crowd mutter that he had already been flogged. The marks were obvious. How weak he must already be. He fell just in front of us. How many other times had he fallen? Perhaps he would die before he reached the place of crucifixion. It would be a blessing.

Maybe one of the guards noticed the way I was looking at him. I do not know why he picked me.

"Hey, you there. Pick up his cross. Now!"

Fear filled my heart as I reached down to pick up the beam. Jesus looked at me and tried to stand. His eyes were framed in dried blood. What had he done to deserve this?

I carried the cross to a barren hill outside the walls of the city. I almost fell once when an onlooker pushed me and spit in my face. I wanted to scream back that I was just an onlooker too, but I realized that I was no longer one of the crowd. I was now part of this strange, cruel drama.

"Turn the other cheek," he had told my sons. Now look at what turning the other cheek had gotten him and me. I wished I could have spit back into the face of the one who had done so to me, but then I heard those taunting words on the lips of my children: "He said to love our enemies, Father."

As I pondered the absurdity of such a statement now, one of the guards screamed into my face,

"Put it here and get out of the way before I find some nails for the likes of you."

My cloak was now torn and bloodstained. I wondered if it was my blood or his. I offered a prayer to whatever god was listening. I wanted to thank some deity that I was not the one being hung up on that piece of wood. "Better his blood than mine," I thought.

As I looked down at the bottom of the hill, I saw the women. I walked toward them. His mother stepped toward me and took my hands, "Oh, thank you for helping him. I hope the cross did not hurt you too much."

I tried to smile and acknowledge her thanks. My use of her

language was not good enough to say what I wanted to say, but then any language was insufficient for this moment.

I stood quietly beside the mother as she watched her son die. I somehow felt I had to stay. The mother of my children was gone, and this poor woman seemed to have no man. The least I could do was stand there with her.

His blood or mine. I kept turning those words over in my mind. I am not sure why. Why had I been chosen? My sons would never believe this story. How painful it would be for me to tell them how I had come to know firsthand of their Jesus.

He tried to say a few things from his cross. What I did hear was as foolish as some of the other things he had said.

"Father, forgive them . . . they know not what they do."

This poor fool. They knew exactly what they were doing. They were doing their cruel job. They were ridding the State of a troublemaker. That was what they were doing.

I had compassion for the mother when Jesus seemed to call on his father. How she must feel hearing him call on a father who was not there! Perhaps he was wishing for his father. I hoped in that moment that his father was dead. How cruel it would be for a husband to leave his wife alone to watch their son die like this.

He said other things, but I missed most of the words because some of the onlookers kept screaming at him. Why did they feel the need to be so cruel? Had some of them lost money on their bets?

Just before he died I did hear him say something that sounded like "My God, why have you forsaken me?"

Finally some words that made sense. If there was any god around that dark day, he had forsaken this poor man. This dying prophet had no god on his side that day. He died without his god. He died without his father. What had my boys seen in this poor man?

Jesus looked toward his mother and toward me and almost in a whisper said, "It is accomplished."

Accomplished? What had been accomplished? Where were his followers? Then I realized how grateful I was that they were not there. Were my own sons in hiding with the rest of his followers?

Surely now my boys would forget this foolish man's words. What did he mean by "accomplished"? In the right moment I will question Alexander and Rufus, for now we have something in common.

As I walked away from that place of death, I again looked at my sleeve and wondered, "His blood or mine?"

Scripture Index